The Best of Cooking with Caramel

Manon Thomas

PREFACE OF THE PUBLISHER

We are pleased that you have chosen this book.
If you are in possession of a paperback book, we will
gladly send you the same as an e-book, then you can
easily turn the pages digitally as well as normally.

We attach great importance to the fact that all of our
authors, when creating their own cookbooks, have
recooked all of their recipes several times.
Therefore, the quality of the design of the recipes and the in-
structions for recooking are detailed and will certainly succeed.

Our authors strive to optimize your recipes, but
tastes are and will always be different!

We at Mindful Publishing support the creation of
the books, so that the creative authors of the recipes
can take their time and enjoy cooking.

We appreciate your opinion about our recipes, so
we would appreciate your review of the book and
your experience with these great recipes!

In order to reduce the printing costs of our books and to
offer the possibility to offer recipes in books at all, we
have to do without pictures in the cookbooks. The digital
version has the same content as the paperback.

Our recipes will convince you and reveal to you

a culinary style you can't get enough of!

Enough of the foreword, let the recipes begin!

CHOCOLATE CARAMEL MOUSSE WITH SALTED BUTTER

Average level

Ingredients

200g of dark chocolate with 64% cacao
100g powdered sugar
60g of buttered butter
10cl of liquid cream
6 eggs

Preparation

Separate the egg whites from the yolks. Beat the whites until stiff and set aside in the refrigerator.
Caramelize the dry sugar in a large saucepan over very low heat. The result should be a blond to light brown caramel.
Bring the cream to the boil.
As soon as it boils, add it to the caramel. If agglomerates or crystals form, raise the heat very slightly and mix continuously, it will melt naturally without recolouring. But be careful not to boil again!
Add the butter cut in small dices.
Melt the chocolate very gently in a bain-marie.
Off the heat, add the egg yolks, then the salted butterscotch. If the consistency is a little too thick, relax with 5 cl of boiling liquid cream.

Pour the chocolate into a bowl.
Gently fold in the egg whites.
Pour the mousse into individual ramekins and store
in the refrigerator for at least two hours.

CHOCOLATE TRUFFLES WITH CARAMEL CHIPS

very easy

Ingredients

200g of dark pastry chocolate
15cl of fresh cream
25g of butter
10 hard caramel candies
Bitter cocoa powder or chocolate vermicelli

Preparation

Crush the caramels to obtain small pieces.
In a double boiler: melt the chocolate then
add the fresh cream and butter.
When everything is melted, add the caramel chips.
Leave to cool.
When the dough has hardened, form balls with the chocolate
and roll them either in bitter cocoa or in chocolate vermicelli.

MUFFIN WITH CARAMEL HEART

easy

Ingredients

200g of dark pastry chocolate
90g of butter
40g of sugar
90g of flour
1/2 bag of baking powder
3 eggs

Preparation

Melt the chocolate and butter in a saucepan. Then put
the mixture in a salad bowl and add the eggs, whisking
vigorously. Then add the sugar, yeast and flour. To mix.
Bake for 20 minutes at 170°C (thermostat 6) in muffin
boxes, themselves in rigid moulds of the same size. Fill
them halfway. When they come out of the oven, remove
the muffins from their boxes and let them cool down.
In a saucepan, make a dry caramel: over low heat, put sugar in the
bottom of a saucepan and wait for it to liquefy and brown. Mix
well with a wooden spoon. Add sugar little by little according
to the desired quantity (you can also add two to three pinches of
salt and a little lemon juice so that the caramel does not blacken).
Meanwhile, in another saucepan, heat the cream over
low heat and add it to the caramel when it is hot and mix
immediately. (Do not put the cold cream in the hot caramel

as there could be splashes) Put back a little bit on the heat so that the mixture becomes homogeneous. Allow to cool.
For the dressing: using an apple corer, make a hole in the middle of the muffins and place them on a plate. Put the caramel cream in a piping bag and fill the hole. You can also decorate the plate with strawberries and caramel decorations (caramel cage ...).

CHOCOLATE CANDIED PEAR AND ITS CARAMEL

easy

Ingredients

200g of pastry chocolate
4 medium sized ripe pears
1/2 l of water
200g of brown sugar
2 tablespoons of fresh cream

Preparation

Peel the pears keeping the tail.
In a high rimmed saucepan, melt the chocolate in pieces with
the water and sugar, bring to a boil. When the chocolate is well
melted, reduce the heat and simmer the pears for 45 minutes.
Take the pears out, drain them carefully and put
them in the refrigerator on the serving plates.
Just before serving, boil the cooking liquid, taking care that
it does not overflow. At the first signs of caramelization,
add fresh cream and boil again for a few moments.
Pour this hot chocolate caramel over the cold pears and enjoy.

MILLE-FEUILLES
CARAMEL AND PEARS

easy

Ingredients

200g of chocolate-caramel
15cl of fresh cream
20 dry cookies
10cl of coffee
1 pear
1 sachet of vanilla sugar

Preparation

Melt the caramel and add the fresh cream to obtain
a homogeneous, slightly fluid paste.
Soak the cookies with coffee.
Alternate in a dish or cookie cutter cookie, caramel,
cookie, caramel, cookie, caramel.
Leave to cool for 12 hours in the refrigerator.
Before serving, cut the pears into small squares and
caramelize them in a pan with the vanilla sugar.
Put the pear cubes on top of the mille-feuilles and serve.

QUICK FRUIT CAKE WITH ITS FRUIT CARAMEL

very easy

Ingredients

200g of flour
100g of sugar
1 sachet of baking powder
3 small jars of cottage cheese
1 large can of fruit salad.
50g melted butter

Preparation

Preheat the oven to 200°.
Mix the flour, sugar, yeast, cottage cheese and melted
butter with the fruit salad without its syrup.
Pour the mixture into a cake tin, butter and flour.
Put in the oven lowered to 180°.
Meanwhile heat the sugar in a saucepan WITHOUT
WATER. Once the sugar has melted and turned
brown, add some of the fruit salad syrup.
Once the brown/red mixture has melted, add the liquid cream.
Serve the cooled cake topped with its caramel.

CHOCOLATE CARAMEL SLICE

easy

Ingredients

200g of flour
100g brown sugar
50g of coconut
125g of butter (melted)

Preparation

Preheat the oven to 180°C (thermostat 6). Butter
THEN put baking paper in a rectangular dish.
BASE: Mix all the ingredients of the BASE in a bowl. Put
the mixture in the dish and then cup (with a spoon).
Put in the oven for 15-20min (-> golden).
Put all the ingredients from the ENVIRONMENT in
a saucepan over medium heat. Cook while whisking
for 8 min (-> golden or boiling). Pour on the BASE and
put in the fridge for 3-4H (-> firm consistency).
ICEING: Put the vegetaline and the chocolate in a double
boiler. Stir and when everything is melted, pour over the
preparation. Harden the icing by putting the caramel
slice in the fridge. Do the same to preserve it.

BRETON CARAMEL CAKE

Average level

Ingredients

200g of flour
125g of white sugar
50g brown sugar
3 eggs
10cl of thick fresh cream
75g of butter breton (half salt)
1 sachet of baking powder
10cl of water

Preparation

Bring the sugar and water to the boil and cook
until the caramel has a nice golden color.
Add the crème fraîche (watch out for splashes)
and stir briskly immediately.
If the mixture is not homogeneous, put it back on very
low heat until the first signs of boiling while stirring.
Melt the butter in parcels, stirring until the mixture
is homogeneous.
In a bowl, beat the eggs into an omelette.
Add the baking powder, flour, salted butterscotch
and brown sugar one after the other.
Butter a cake tin and pour the dough into it.
Bake in a preheated oven at 210°C (gas mark 7) for 40 minutes.

POACHED APPLE PIE WITH CARAMEL AND RUM

Average level

Ingredients

200g of flour
80g of powdered sugar or powdered sugar
25g of almond powder
1 pinch of salt
120g of butter
1 egg

Preparation

In a salad bowl, mix the flour, salt, powdered sugar
and almond powder. Incorporate the very cold butter
and cut into pieces to make a sandblasting.
Add the beaten egg while working the dough as little as possible.
Leave the dough to rest for at least 1 hour in the fridge.
During this time prepare the caramel: in a thick-bottomed
frying pan, pour the sugar with the 2 tablespoons of water.
Heat over medium heat until the caramel turns brown.
Preheat the oven to 200°C (gas mark 7).
When it is hot, put the dough in the oven for about
10 minutes after pricking it with a fork. Remove and
set aside when the dough is white and dry.
Peel the apples into quarters and throw them into

the caramel. Wait until the caramel becomes smooth again. Stir the pan vigorously to distribute the caramel evenly over the apples. Poach the apples for about ten minutes, then add a good shake of rum and flambé. Continue to spread the caramel-rum mixture over the apples for another 1 to 2 minutes and then place them on the pre-baked dough.
Make the binder by mixing the cream, the egg and the vanilla sugar.
Add the remaining caramel in the pan as a topping and then the binder.
Bake for 15 to 20 minutes.

CHOCOLATE AND CARAMEL TOPPING CAKE

easy

Ingredients

200g of farinex2
3 eggs
50g of sugar
1 sachet of baking powder
1 half of milk

Preparation

Mix the 3 eggs, the sugar, the flour, the yeast, and the milk.
Repeat the operation a second time, changing some
proportions, for the second cake, which will be smaller.
Butter the two moulds (one large and one small)
and pour the preparation into the moulds. Bake
for 40 minutes at 190°C (thermostat 6-7).
Leave to cool and remove from the moulds.
Arrange on a dish, putting the large cake first
and then the small one on top.
Make a caramel and pour it over the cakes.
Melt the chocolate and cream and pour over
the cakes, leaving space for a nut.

CARAMELIZED HAZELNUTS

very easy

Ingredients

200g of hazelnuts
50g of buttered butter
70g of brown sugar
2 tablespoons of water

Preparation

In a small saucepan melt the butter. `
Add the brown sugar. Stir vigorously.
When the caramel clings to the sides of the pan, add
2 tablespoons of water and let it reduce for 1 minute
and 30 minutes over low heat while stirring.
Arrange the hazelnuts in the caramel and turn them in
all directions so that they are well impregnated.
Then place them on a large dish, spacing them out.
Let the caramel harden before moving them.

CARAMEL FONDUE WITH FLEUR DE SEL

very easy

Ingredients

200g of sugar
2 tablespoons of water
100g of butter
2 pinches of fleur de sel
100g of mascarpone

Preparation

Put sugar and water in a saucepan and heat
over high heat without stirring.
As soon as the mixture starts to turn pale, remove from
the heat, add the butter and the fleur de sel and stir with a
wooden spatula - the mixture seems lumpy, it will settle.
Put back on a low heat, add the mascarpone and
stir gently until the mixture is smooth.
Place in a fondue pot and serve immediately.

ORANGE CARAMEL CREAM

Average level

Ingredients

200g of sugar
Orange

Preparation

Preheat the oven to 180°C (thermostat 6).
Prepare the cream by beating the eggs as for an omelette.
Put on very low heat and add the sugar,
then the milk little by little.
When the mixture is homogeneous, bottle it
and shake it for a good 2 minutes.
Add the cointreau to the cream, shake again 30 seconds.
Make a caramel with the sugar and orange juice.
Pour the caramel into the bottom of ramekins in a
layer of 1/2cm thick and cover with cream.
Cook in a bain-marie for 55 minutes.

CARAMEL FLAVOURED MOUSSE

easy

Ingredients

200g powdered sugar
3 eggs
80g of flour
1l of milk
70g of sugar cubes (caramel)

Preparation

Break the eggs and separate the yolks from the whites.
In a salad bowl, mix the flour and the sugar then dig a
fountain. To pour there the yolks of eggs diluted with
a little milk. Bring the rest of the milk to the boil then
incorporate it into the salad bowl, without ceasing to stir.
Pour the contents of the salad bowl into a saucepan, then
thicken the cream over low heat while stirring.
Remove from the heat as soon as it boils and
keep warm in a double boiler.
In another saucepan, prepare a caramel:
Melt the sugar cubes with water and remove from the heat
when the sugar colors as you wish. Cut off the caramel by
pouring a little cold water into the pan while stirring briskly.
Stir the thick caramel into the hot milk and mix
well. Beat the whites into firm snow then add them
delicately to the hot milk flavoured with caramel.

Then pour the caramel cream into ramekins
and set aside in the refrigerator.
To taste quite fresh.

SALTED BUTTERSCOTCH CARAMEL ROLL CAKE

Average level

Ingredients

200g powdered sugar
40g of butter and half salt
20cl of liquid cream
1/2 teaspoon of fleur de sel (or a pinch of ordinary salt) -

Preparation

For the salted butterscotch:
In a large saucepan, melt the sugar until you obtain a brown caramel. Stir the saucepan when the bottom begins to melt to incorporate the sugar that remains on top.
Remove from the heat and stir gently with a spatula, such as a Maryse,
add the butter.
On low heat, add the liquid cream and the fleur de sel.
Mix well until a homogeneous consistency is obtained.
Put, for example, in a jam jar. Cover with cling film and leave to cool for at least 1/2 hour.
For the rolled cake:
Preheat the oven to 210°C (gas mark 7).
Beat 3 egg whites until stiff.
In another bowl, mix the 3 yolks and the

whole egg that you have left.
with powdered sugar and vanilla sugar.
Gradually stir in the flour and baking powder.
Gradually add the egg whites.
Spread the preparation over the entire surface of a
baking tray, previously covered with baking paper.
Put in the oven for 10 minutes.
Once baked, if necessary, remove the cake from the
baking paper by sliding a knife blade in between.
Spread with salted butter caramel and roll.
Hmmmm!

CARAMEL VERRINES

very easy

Ingredients

200g powdered sugar
4 tablespoons of water
4 tablespoons of mascarpone
75g of buttered butter
100g of hazelnuts

Preparation

In a saucepan, melt the sugar and water over very low heat.
As soon as the caramel begins to form, turn the pan to mix
well (turning with a spoon will crystallize the mixture).
Remove from the heat as soon as the caramel
takes a beautiful color.
Add the Mascarpone and the salted butter. Mix well.
At the bottom of the verrines, put some hazelnuts
and pour the preparation over it.
Sprinkle some hazelnut pieces on top for the presentation
and put in the fridge before tasting.

MICROWAVE SALTED BUTTER CARAMEL CREAM

very easy

Ingredients

200g powdered sugar
5cl of water
1 teaspoon of lemon juice
50g of buttered butter
40cl of liquid cream

Preparation

Put the powdered sugar in a glass bowl with the water
and lemon and cover with a special microwave film.
Place in the microwave for 6 to 8 minutes at full
power, depending on the power of the oven.
Stop cooking as soon as the sugar turns a nice caramel color.
Gently remove the film (be careful not to let the caramel
bubble during the whole recipe) and gradually add
the cream and butter, stirring with a spoon.
As soon as you obtain a very homogeneous mixture, put in a jar.

CARAMEL DESSERT CREAM

easy

Ingredients

200g of sugar (in powder or in pieces, at your choice,
180g if you don't like too much sugar)
30g of butter
1/2l milk
30g of cornstarch

Preparation

Put the sugar in a saucepan and sprinkle with a trickle of water.
Boil over high heat, watching carefully, until caramel
forms. When the mixture browns, stir by turning the pan
(without utensil). Always let caramelize over high heat
(without letting it burn, less than a minute is enough).
Remove the pan from the heat.
Prepare the cold milk mixed with the cornstarch separately.
Remove from the heat, add the butter, mix with a fork,
then gradually add the milk - cornstarch mixture,
stirring constantly with a fork.
Return to medium heat. Boil the mixture
until it thickens, stirring regularly.
Pour into jars, allow to cool and then put
in the fridge to enjoy cold!

APRICOT CARAMEL CAKE

very easy

Ingredients

20 abricots-fresh
4 eggs
200g of butter
200g powdered sugar
200g of flour
about 5g of baking powder
2 tablespoons of rum
2 pinches of salt

Preparation

Start with the caramel: in a saucepan, heat the sugar cubes and water over medium heat. As soon as the caramel is well browned but not yet brown, pour immediately into the pan, spreading it well on all sides. Leave to cool. Clean and stone the apricots. Cut them in half and arrange them in the mould, cut side up. Work the softened butter and powdered sugar in a bowl until a smooth paste is obtained. Gradually stir in the eggs, flour, baking powder, rum and salt. Pour the dough over the fruit and bake in a preheated oven at 180-210°C (gas mark 6/7) for approx. 45 minutes. Unmould the cake while it is still warm, but serve it cold.

SMALL CARAMEL AND COCONUT MILK CREAMS TOPPED WITH BANANAS

Average level

Ingredients

20 pieces of white sugar
15cl of water

Preparation

Turn on the oven at 180°C and while it is heating,
make a caramel.
Place the sugar in pieces in a thick-bottomed saucepan,
pour the 15 cl of water and cook over low heat until
the melted sugar turns a reddish color.
To homogenize, shake the handle of the pan.
Pour the caramel into the bottom of 6 lightly buttered ramekins.
For the creams :
Pour normal milk and coconut milk into a saucepan,
heat this mixture over medium heat until it boils.
Meanwhile, place the 3 whole eggs and the 4 yolks in a bowl.
Add 100 g of brown sugar and beat until the mixture clears up.
Pour the boiling milk, mix well and filter over a bowl.
Pour the mixture obtained into the 6 ramekins, over the caramel.

Cover each ramekin with aluminum foil.
Cook them in a bain-marie in the oven (with
the aluminium foil) for 20 minutes.
When the preparation is cooked, let it cool down,
then place in the fridge for a few hours.
Before serving:
Peel the bananas and cut them into slices.
Brown them for one minute per side in a frying
pan with a little butter.
Sprinkle each side with the remaining brown sugar.
Turn out the contents of each ramekin onto a plate.
Decorate with the warm banana slices and
fresh mint leaves rinsed with water.
Serve immediately.

COOKIES CARAMEL HEART

very easy

Ingredients

220g of flour
120g of semi-salted butter
100g of sugar
1 egg
1 teaspoon baking powder
50g of chocolate

Preparation

Preheat the oven to 180°C (thermostat 6).
Beat the egg with the sugar and soft butter.
Add the flour and the yeast. Mix well.
Incorporate the chocolate chips.
Form balls of dough between your hands, dig the ball of
dough to put 1 teaspoon of caramel and close well.
Place the cookie balls on a baking sheet
covered with baking paper.
Space the cookies from each other, they
will spread out during baking.
Put them in the oven for 12 minutes. The cookies
should not color, they will harden as they cool.

SOFT CARAMEL AND CHOCOLATE CAKE

very easy

Ingredients

225g of dark chocolate
150g powdered sugar
130g of butter (dare the half-salt!)
4 eggs

Preparation

Turn on the oven at thermostat 6.
Melt the chocolate in a bain-marie
In a saucepan, make caramel with the sugar and a little water.
Remove from the heat and gradually add the butter
cut into pieces, add the melted chocolate and
then insert the egg yolks one by one.
Whisk the egg whites until stiff. Incorporate
them delicately into the preparation.
Butter and flour a 22cm mould and pour the preparation into it.
Cook for 25 minutes.
Turn out hot and eat cold.

CARAMEL AND CHOCOLATE FONDANT

very easy

Ingredients

230g of dark chocolate
150g of butter
9 tablespoons of caramel liquid
5 eggs

Preparation

1) Preheating of the furnace 180°C.
2) Bring the caramel to the boil over low heat,
then add the butter and dark chocolate.
3) Mix everything off the heat to obtain a smooth dough.
4) Separate and whisk the egg whites.
5) Add one by one the yolks into the choco-caramel dough.
6) Mix the whites and the dough.
7) Pour into a mold or into buttered ramekins.
Put in the oven for 20 minutes.

CHOCOLATE FONDANT WITH SALTED BUTTER CARAMEL SAUCE

easy

Ingredients

240g of dark chocolate
4 eggs + 4 yolks
200g of butter
200g powdered sugar
70g of flour
30cl of fresh half-thick cream
50g of semi-salted butter
6 slices of fresh pineapple
6 scoops of vanilla ice cream

Preparation

Preheat the oven for about 15 minutes at 200°C (thermostat 6-7).
Break the chocolate into small pieces and melt it in
the microwave with 4 tablespoons of water.
Add the soft butter cut into small pieces to the chocolate
mixture and mix gently with a wooden spatula.
In a salad bowl, beat the whole eggs, egg yolks and
100 g sugar until the mixture whitens.
Add the warm chocolate and flour and mix vigorously.
Pour the dough into sillicone muffin tins.
Put in the oven and bake for 13 minutes

at 200°C (thermostat 6-7).
Turn out the still warm fondants.
For the salted butterscotch: pour 100 g caster sugar
and 1 tablespoon of water into a saucepan.
Cook the caramel.
As soon as the caramel has blonded, add the 30 cl of
slightly warm crème fraîche (it is better incorporated)
and mix gently over low heat.
Turn off the heat, add the 50 g of salted butter and mix gently.
To serve: place on each individual plate, a fondant, a slice
of fresh pineapple, a scoop of vanilla ice cream, sprinkle
with caramel sauce and decorate with whipped cream.

COOKIES WHITE CHOCOLATE CARAMEL

very easy

Ingredients

250g of butter
60g of sugar
60g brown sugar
2 eggs
350g of flour
1 teaspoon of yeast powder
100g of white chocolate
75g of caramel
Salt

Preparation

Work the soft butter with the two sugars until
a homogeneous mixture is obtained.
Add the eggs and mix well.
Add the sifted flour, salt and baking powder and mix again.
Add the chocolate chips and caramel.
Preheat the oven to 180°C (gas mark 6) and cover the tray
with baking paper. Using two teaspoons, place small heaps
of dough worth a walnut. Remember to space them well
apart as the dough will spread out quite strongly.
Put in the oven and leave to cook for about ten minutes.
Remember that cookies harden as they cool.

PEACH AND CARAMEL CAKE

easy

Ingredients

250g of butter
60g of cane sugar
825g of natural peach in a box
250g powdered sugar
3 teaspoons of lemon
3 lightly beaten eggs
310g of flour, sifted (wheat flour for baking for example)
250g plain yoghurt

Preparation

Preheat the oven to 180°C. Grease a 23 cm diameter
mould and flour it.
Melt 50 g of butter and sprinkle the base
of the mould with cane sugar.
Drain the peaches, reserving 1 tablespoon of juice
and spread in the mould, curved side down.
Cream the remaining butter with the sugar and lemon zest for 5
to 6 minutes using an electric mixer until the mixture whitens.
Gradually add the eggs, beating well after each addition.
Using a metal spoon, add the flour, alternating with
the yoghurt and the reserved peach juice.
Spread the preparation obtained in the mould, smooth the
surface and bake in the oven until the tip of a knife pricked

in the center comes out without any trace of dough.
Leave to cool for 30 minutes and unmould on a serving dish.
Enjoy your meal.

TIRAMISU CARAMEL AND SUEDE

easy

Ingredients

250g of mascarpone
3 eggs
75g of powdered sugar
1 sachet of vanilla sugar
1 packet of cookies with a spoon (24 cookies minimum)
200g of caramel coulisde
10 Supper

Preparation

Separate the whites from the yolks.
Mount the whites into snow.
In a bowl mix the powdered sugar and the yolks with the
vanilla sugar, then add the mascarpone, then add the egg
whites and stir gently so as not to break the whites.
The machine is ready.
Then mix the caramel coulis with a little water to
allow the cookies to absorb the liquid.
Dip the cookies in the caramel and place a first layer in the dish,
place the appliance on the first layer and repeat a second time.
Then mix the suede to arrange them on the tiramisu.
And place in a cool place.
Enjoy!

VERRINE TIRAMISU SPECULOOS CARAMEL SALTED BUTTER

easy

Ingredients

250g of mascarpone
50g of semi-salted butter
20cl of liquid cream
3 egg trails
150g powdered sugar
Speculoos

Preparation

Heat the sugar in a saucepan until you get a caramel.
Add the butter off the heat and then the warm cream.
Return to the heat if necessary to obtain a smooth caramel.
Separate the whites from the yolks.
Whisk the whites to snow with a pinch of salt.
Mix the yolks with the mascarpone.
Gently add your whites.
Pour part of your caramel into a plate.
Then you dip your cookies one by one in the caramel
and crumble them roughly.
In a verrine you deposit a layer of cookie cover with mascarpone
preparation a new layer of cookies finally a layer of mascarpone.
You put in the fridge at least 3 hours before serving

and cover with the rest of the caramel.
And there you settle down and succumb to the delight
of this tiramisu!

APRICOT POUND CAKE ON A BED OF CARAMEL

easy

Ingredients

250g of sugar
15cl of water

Preparation

Prepare the caramel, put the water then the sugar in a saucepan,
let it color without stirring until the caramel has an amber color.
Then place the caramel at the bottom of your
cake tin over the entire surface.
Once the caramel covers the bottom of the dish, arrange the
apricots on top of the caramel to cover the bottom of the dish.
Then prepare the cake batter.
Mix the eggs and sugar in a dish, add the flour
and baking powder and mix again.
Finally add the oil, mix it all together and
spread the dough over the apricots.
Bake for 15 to 20 minutes, thermostat 6 of your oven.

CARAMEL TO
BE TOPPED

easy

Ingredients

250g caster sugar
20cl of liquid cream
50g of butter

Preparation

Put the sugar in a medium saucepan over low heat. Do
not mix the sugar with a spatula but turn the pan on itself
a few times so that the unmelted sugar can melt.
When the sugar has melted completely, add the liquid
cream and immediately remove from the heat.
Without wasting time, add the butter and
turn the saucepan again.
When the mixture becomes homogeneous,
let the caramel cool down.

THOUSAND SHEETS SPECULOOS CARAMEL SALTED BUTTER WITH CARAMELIZED APPLES

Average level

Ingredients

250g caster sugar
60g of butter and half salt
25cl thick cream
50cl of liquid cream30
400g of speculoos
2 apples golden
8g of gelatin
30g of brown sugar
5cl of rum

Preparation

Make the salted butterscotch caramel.
Put 150 g of caster sugar to caramelize.
When the preparation is brown enough, remove the pan from
the fire and incorporate the butter half salt in small pieces.
Then, put back on soft fire and add the thick cream,
mix delicately to homogenize the preparation.
Put the gelatine leaves (8g) to soften in cold water,

then add them to the preparation.
Whip the liquid cream into whipped cream.
When the salted butter caramel sauce is rather tepid, incorporate
it into the whipped cream delicately using a spatula.
Cut the golden apples into half slices and brown
them in a pan with the brown sugar.
Prepare a syrup with 100 g caster sugar, 2 dl water and the rum.
Take a mould with fairly high walls and line it with cling film.
Begin by placing the speculoos previously soaked in
the syrup at the bottom of the mould nicely thinking
that the visible side of the cake is at the bottom.
Alternating layers of caramel mousse with
salted butter and speculoos by incorporating the
apples in the middle of the assembly.
Leave to cool for 4 hours in the refrigerator.
Unmould and serve.

APPLE AND CARAMEL NUGGETS FLAN CAKE

easy

Ingredients

250g brewed yoghurt 0%.
250g of flour
40g vanilla sugar
2 eggs
100g of applesauce
4 apples
1 sachet of baking powder

Preparation

Peel apples, remove cores and seeds and cut into strips.
Preheat the oven to 180°C.
In a salad bowl, whisk the eggs with the sugar and the
compote, add the yeast, then the yoghurts.
Add the flour in 3 or 4 times.
Add the apple slices, mix them and break them a little
to make it easier to coat them with the dough.
Add the caramel nuggets and mix.
Pour the mixture into a buttered baking
pan and bake for 45 minutes.

CHOCOLATE-CHANTILLY-CARAMEL PROFITEROLES

Average level

Ingredients

25cl of water
1/2 teaspoon of salt
1 tablespoon of caster sugar
150g of flour
60g of butter
4 eggs

Preparation

The dough :
Put the water, butter, salt and sugar in a saucepan. Bring to a boil.
When it boils, pour in the flour all at once and
stir. A ball of dough will form.
Take the pan off the heat and put the eggs into
the dough, stirring after each egg.
Butter and line a baking sheet and put small balls of dough on it.
Cook until the balls are puffed up and golden brown.
For the whipped cream:
Put the sugar and cream in a bowl.
In another bowl put cold water and ice cubes.
Put the bowl with cream and sugar in the
bowl with water and ice cubes.

Beat with an electric mixer.
The cream is finished when it becomes frothy
and forms beaks at the end of the whips.
Put it in a cool place.
The caramel :
Put the sugar in a saucepan.
Add a drop of lemon juice.
Add half a glass of water.
When the mixture makes bubbles, remove the pan from the heat.
Wait for the caramel to cool.
When the caramel has cooled, put it in a plastic bowl.
The chocolate :
Melt the chocolate and butter in the microwave.
Take it out and put it in a plastic bowl.
When your cabbages are ready, let them cool and then cut
the top off and put a spoonful of whipped cream in it. Dip
half of the cabbage in the caramel and the other half in the
chocolate. Put them on a nice plate and serve them!
Bon appétit:D

ALMOND CARAMEL CAKE

Average level

Ingredients

25cl of hot water
1 teaspoon baking soda
250g of almondentières but that you will cut
in 2 (almonds without the skin)
75g of butter
300g of flour
1/2 teaspoon of salt
1 teaspoon of yeast
220g powdered sugar
1 sachet of vanilla sugar
1 egg
5 spoonfuls of brown sugar
2 tablespoons of butter
2 tablespoons of fresh cream

Preparation

Boil the water, plunge the almonds 5 min by lowering
the fire a little.
After cooking, add the bicarbonate of soda.
Meanwhile, mix the softened butter, flour, salt and yeast,
then the sugar, vanilla and beaten egg. Mix well.
Add lastly the baking soda water and almonds and mix.
Put in a cake tin and then in the oven at

180°, thermostat 6, for 30 min.
Leave to cool, and then just make the caramel.
The caramel: mix the brown sugar, butter and cream.
Bring to the boil and cook while stirring for 3 minutes:
the caramel should have a nice dark brown color.
When the caramel is lukewarm (but still soft), spread over the
cake with a spatula. The caramel will then harden on the cake,
a cake like no other and delicious...

CARAMEL PIE WITH SALTED BUTTER

Average level

Ingredients

25cl of whipping cream
150g of sugar
60g of semi-salted butter
1 shortbread paste

Preparation

Preheat your oven to 180°C (thermostat 6).
Line a mould with a shortbread pastry.
Gently prick the dough to prevent it from swelling and
bake it at 180°C for about 30 minutes (take it out of
the oven when it takes a slightly golden color).
Let it cool down.
While it cools, prepare the appliance:
Put the sugar and cream in a saucepan and bring
to the boil while stirring regularly.
Maintain this boiling while continuing to stir for
about half an hour until the mixture takes on a
pasty consistency (a bit like custard).
At this point, add the butter and continue to cook
for 5/10 minutes until the desired consistency is
obtained. To test the consistency, place a few drops of
the mixture on a cold plate from time to time.
When the preparation takes a light blond color and

stands sufficiently on the plate, remove from the heat and
pour immediately on the already baked tart base.
Leave to cool and put in the fridge for at least 2 hours.

VANILLA/CARAMEL ICE CREAM

very easy

Ingredients

25cl whole milk
2 eggs
100g powdered sugar
45cl of liquid cream
1/2 vanilla bean
2 tablespoons of liquid caramel topping

Preparation

In a saucepan over low heat, heat the milk,
eggs and sugar while stirring.
Remove the seeds from the vanilla bean
and add it to the preparation.
As soon as the mixture obtains the consistency of a thick
custard, remove from the heat and leave to cool.
Add the liquid cream and place in the fridge overnight.
Place in an ice-cream maker for 30 minutes and transfer to tubs.
Pour liquid caramel on top and using a pick (with a
skewer for example), mix gently to zebra the ice cream
(but not too much otherwise the caramel will mix
with the ice cream which will become brown).
Put in the freezer.

PUMPKIN CARAMEL CHEESECAKE

Average level

Ingredients

260g of chocolate cookietout
50g of melted butter
3 eggs
500g of ricotta
125g of fresh goat cheese
400g of pumpkin puree
100g of brown sugar

Preparation

The day before: preparation of the cheesecake
Preheat the oven to 160° (thermostat 5-6).
Place the all chocolate cookies in a freezer bag. Close the bag
and crush the cookies with a rolling pin (or a glass bottle).
Melt the butter in the microwave. Mix the butter
and the crushed cookies.
Line the bottom of a 24 to 26 cm diameter springform
pan with this preparation. To pack well.
In a bowl beat the ricotta and cheese with the eggs using a
mixer. Add the pumpkin puree and brown sugar. Beat again.
Pour this mixture into the pan on the cookie dough base.
Put in the oven and bake for 40 minutes.
In the meantime, mix in a bowl with your fingertips the butter,
sugar, almond powder and flour until you get big crumbs.

Take the cheesecake out of the oven, sprinkle with streusel,
put in the oven again and bake for another 10 minutes.
Turn off the oven and let the cheesecake cool. Keep the oven door
closed for several hours. Afterwards keep in the refrigerator for
at least 10 hours (the day before or the day before is even better).

MELTING APPLES WITH SALTED BUTTERSCOTCH CARAMEL ON BRETON PUCK

easy

Ingredients

280g of buttered butter
4 egg yolks
385g of sugar
280g of flour
30cl of liquid cream
5 apples cut into quarters
1 sachet of baking powder

Preparation

Preparation of Breton shortbread :
Sand 160 G of salted butter in the 280 G of flour.
Beside, beat the egg yolks, the yeast and 160 g of sugar until the
mixture whitens. Pour this mixture in the flour and the butter.
Knead until obtaining a beautiful ball of dough quite homoge-
neous. Spread it with the roller so as to have a good thickness.
Using a cookie cutter, cut out circles of 12cm in diameter

(here a Lego plastic glass from McDonald's).
Bake for 10 minutes at 180°C (thermostat 6) so that they are just
golden brown. Take them out of the oven and reserve for later.
Preparation of the caramel salted butter:
In a saucepan melt the remaining 120 g of salted butter. When it
is liquid, add the remaining 225 g of sugar then let brown while
stirring until it thickens. Then add the 30 cl of liquid cream and
let cook 2/3 minutes then remove from heat and reserve.
Preparation of the melting apples:
Make brown your apples in quarter in the quantity
of salted butter that you will judge necessary.
When they are well gilded, add half of the salted butterscotch
caramel realized previously. Reserve your apples.
To prepare your dessert:
In a dessert plate, place a Breton shortbread,
cover it with your caramelized apples, taking care to leave
the edge visible. Coat with caramel as you wish.
Pour a small amount of caramel into an espresso
cup and place it on your plate.

CARAMEL ROYAL

easy

Ingredients

2 egg whites
45g of sugar
45g of almond powder
45g of powdered sugar
15g of flour

Preparation

La Dacquoise: Preheat the oven to 180°C (thermostat 6).
Beat the whites by adding the sugar in several times.
Mix the almond powder, powdered sugar and flour. Gently mix this mixture with the whites using a spatula.
Place a small rectangular or round frame on a silpat. Spread the dough inside the frame. Bake for about 13 minutes and let cool.
Chocolate crunch:
Melt the praline in the microwave for 1-2 minutes.
Crumble the gavottes and mix with the praline. Place this mixture on the dacquoise. Set aside in a cool place.
Chocolate mousse:
Whip the cream into a whipped cream (the cream should be put in the fridge beforehand for a better grip). Melt the caramel chocolate in a bain-marie. Incorporate the chocolate into the cream. Cover the dacquoise with the mixture and set aside in the fridge.

PINEAPPLE CARAMEL CAKE

very easy

Ingredients

2 tins of pineapple
6 eggs
2 lemons
40g of flour
Caramel liquid
200g powdered sugar

Preparation

Line a mould with caramel, cover the bottom
with pineapple slices.
Mix 8 pineapple slices. Cook the purée obtained
with the 200 g of sugar for 4 min.
Add the rest of the pineapples cut in pieces and continue
cooking for 3 min.
In a salad bowl, mix the flour and the eggs, add the pineapple
puree and the juice of the 2 lemons. Pour into the mould.
Cook 1 h at 180°C, thermostat 6. Let cool at least 10 h.

MEXICAN CARAMEL CREAM

easy

Ingredients

2 cans of sweetened condensed milk
Milk
5 eggs
2 vanilla beans
4 fresh and fragrant green lemons
10 tablespoons of sugar + a little water

Preparation

Prepare the milk: in a saucepan, pour the cans of
condensed milk and the equivalent of a milk can.
Remove the zest from the limes, and split the vanilla
beans by removing them with the tip of a knife.
Put everything in the saucepan and heat; turn off the
heat to boiling and macerate for 20 minutes.
Prepare a caramel: put the sugar and half a glass of water
in a mould and melt on the heat of the plate.
When the caramel takes on a nice amber color, remove and
tilt the mold so that the caramel spreads on the sides.
Beat the eggs and through a sieve, pour in the milk.
At first a small quantity, and mix well at the same time
and vigorously to avoid coagulation of the egg yolks.
Pour in the rest of the milk and mix.
Pour into the mould and bake for 1 hour in a

hot oven preheated in a bain-marie.
Leave to cool, put in the fridge and unmould.
A pure moment of delight and an in-ra-ta-ble dessert!!!!

CARAMEL APPLE LIKE A LOVE APPLE

very easy

Ingredients

2 tablespoons of milk
4 apples (Pink Lady type)
200g of soft candy caramel
Hazelnuts/crushed nuts

Preparation

Wash apples well.
In a salad bowl, pour the caramels and sprinkle them with milk.
Melt in the microwave for 30 seconds, then 30 seconds
more if necessary.
Coarsely crush the hazelnuts with a knife or in a food
processor, then set aside in a soup plate.
Prick the apples on a wooden stick and dip them in
the caramel so that they are well coated.
Roll the bottom of the apples in the crushed hazelnuts and
place on a baking sheet covered with baking paper.
To vary the pleasures, you can also dip the apples in grated
coconut, chocolate shavings, small sweet vermicelli?

TRADITIONAL CARAMEL CUSTARD

easy

Ingredients

2g of crystallized sugar
1/2l whole milk
4 eggs
1/2 vanilla bean
Water

Preparation

Prepare the caramel :
In a small saucepan, simmer 1 dl of water and 75 g of sugar.
Turn frequently with a wooden spoon.
Meanwhile....
Prepare the cream:
Boil the milk, the rest of the sugar and the vanilla
bean cut in half lengthwise.
Remove from the heat and add the 4 beaten (whole)
eggs to the preparation. Mix everything together.
When your caramel is golden, pour it into a Pyrex
dish. Then pour the cream over it.
Bake the dish in the BAIN-MARIE in an oven
at 180°C for 20 to 30 minutes.
Check the cooking with the tip of a knife. It must come
out dry after having been planted in the flan.
Leave to cool.

DRINKING YOGHURT WITH CREAMY CARAMEL COULIS IN THE YOGHURT MAKER

easy

Ingredients

2l semi-skimmed cow's milk
1 natural yogurt or 1 sachet of ferments
200g of cane sugar
6 tablespoons of water
20cl of liquid cream
Vegetable cream or other vegetable cream

Preparation

To prepare the caramel, mix water and sugar in
a saucepan. Heat over medium heat.
The sugar will begin to caramelize after a few minutes of
cooking. Watch the cooking carefully, especially as it begins to
darken. Turn off the heat as soon as the sugar begins to brown.
Add the cream (at room temperature or slightly
heated, to avoid thermal shock and caramel splashes)
and stir to obtain a homogeneous caramel.
Place 1/2 teaspoon of creamy caramel in each bottle.
In a large bowl, mix the milk and the yoghurt or ferment

packet, then whisk until the mixture is homogeneous.
Spread the mixture in the containers over the caramel.
Place them in the yoghurt maker and cook in yoghurt
mode for 6 hours.
Once the program is finished, close the bottles if not already done
and place them in the refrigerator for a minimum of 4 hours.
Shake vigorously before consumption.

CRUNCHY CARAMEL OR CHOCOLATE TIRAMISU

easy

Ingredients

2 eggs
50g of fine sugar
250g of mascarpone
12 cookies with a spoon
3 sheets of brick
Brown sugar and brown sugar
Chocolate powder (or caramel)
10cl of milk

Preparation

Separate the whites from the yolks.
Blanch the egg yolks with the fine sugar.
Add the mascarpone to the previous preparation.
Beat the egg whites until stiff and add them gently to the
previous preparation (egg yolks, sugar and mascarpone).
Take the sheets of brick pastry, sprinkle them with
brown sugar or brown sugar and put them in the oven
until they are golden brown. Crumble them.
Mix the caramel or chocolate powder with the milk.
Dip the cookies spoonfuls into the milk caramel
or milk chocolate.

Then put the spoon cookies in the bottom of a dish.
Put half of the mascarpone mixture on the spoon cookies.
Put the crumbled brick pastry sheets on top.
Put the rest of the mascarpone preparation on the cookies spoon.
Chill for at least 2 hours.
Then taste. Enjoy your meal.

CHEESECAKE, CHOCOLATE AND CARAMEL (QUEBEC)

Average level

Ingredients

2 packages of soft Canadian cream cheese
1/2 cup of granulated sugar
2/3 cup of cream at 35%.
1/2 cup of cream
3 beaten eggs
1 tablespoon of flour
1 cup of butterscotch

Preparation

Preheat oven to 325°F (160°C).
Using an electric mixer, blend all ingredients, except
caramel chips, until smooth and even.
Pour half of the mixture into the cake pan containing
the chocolate pie crust.
Spread caramel chips evenly over batter and
cover with remaining batter.
Bake for 45 to 50 minutes in the oven or until a
toothpick inserted in the dough comes out clean.
Remove from the oven and wait 15 minutes before unmoulding.
Garnish the cake or each individual portion with
caramel sauce and serve immediately.

Chocolate pie crust:
In a bowl, mix all ingredients with a fork.
With this mixture, line the bottom and sides of
a buttered round removable-wall pan.
Set aside.
Caramel sauce :
In a small saucepan, melt butter and sugar for 2 minutes, stirring
regularly. Stir in the water and bring to a boil while stirring.
Reduce heat and simmer until a smooth,
golden syrup is obtained.
Remove from heat and set aside.

APPLE AND CARAMEL MILLE-FEUILLES

easy

Ingredients

2 pre-spread flaky pastry (commercially available)
4 apples golden or baking apples
Caramel with salted butter or milk jam
20g of butter
2 tablespoons of sugar
1 tablespoon powdered sugar

Preparation

- Preheat the oven to 220°, thermostat 7-8.
- Cut out rectangles of about 4x10 cm from the puff pastry. You need 3 rectangles per individual mille-feuille, so 12 rectangles in all.
- Place the rectangles on baking paper on a baking tray, spaced 1 cm apart (they will swell slightly so they can touch each other) and bake for 20 min at 220°, gas mark 7-8.
- In the meantime, peel and cut the apples into strips (about 1 cm thick).
- In a frying pan over medium heat, melt the butter and add the apples. Brown them and continue cooking by sprinkling with sugar.
- When the puff pastry rectangles are cooked, place one rectangle in each plate (4), then cover with a layer of caramel (as you would do for jam on toast) and apple slices. Cover with a second

rectangle, repeat the operation and finish with a rectangle.
- Sprinkle with powdered sugar.

TRIFLES PEARS SPECULOOS CARAMEL WITH SALTED BUTTER AND MASCARPONE

easy

Ingredients

2 pears
1/2l of water
50g of sugar
1/2 vanilla bean

Preparation

In a saucepan, heat the water, the 50 g of
sugar and 1/2 vanilla pod.
Boil gently for about 10 minutes.
During this time, peel and cut the pears, add them
to the syrup and leave to cook for 1/4 hour.
At the end of the cooking time, let the pears
cool in the syrup for about 1 hour.
Mix the cottage cheese, mascarpone and
50 g caster sugar with a whisk.
Reserve in the fridge.
Crush the speculoos with the manual masher.
Divide the crushed speculoos in 4 large verrines or cups.

Cut the cooled pears into pieces.
Add salted butterscotch caramel on top of the pears,
about one tablespoon in each verrine.
Add the mascarpone and cheese mixture to each verrine.
You can add chocolate vermicelli for decoration.
Put in the fridge for at least two hours.

EASY VERRINE PEAR AND CARAMEL SALTED BUTTER

very easy

Ingredients

2 pears
1 yourt velouté
2 Swiss children
8 speculoos
1 jar of salted butter caramel
2 tablespoons of sugar

Preparation

Crumble the speculoos with a pestle and
place at the bottom of the glasses.
Mix the velvety yoghurt and the petits suisses
and sweeten. Spread over the speculoos.
Peel and cut the pears into small pieces. Arrange in the verrines.
Put the salted butterscotch on the pears at your convenience.
Enjoy!

VERRINES WITH PEARS AND LIGHT CREAM SALTED BUTTERSCOTCH CARAMEL

very easy

Ingredients

2 ripe pears
1/2l milk
2g agar-agar
70g of buttered butter
70g of sugar

Preparation

Wash, peel and dice the pears.
Dissolve the agar-agar in the milk and heat on very low heat.
Meanwhile, prepare the caramel: in a saucepan, put the sugar
wetted with a tablespoon of water and the butter, heat over
high heat until you obtain a caramel of a deep brown.
Keep off the heat.
Bring the milk with the agar-agar to the boil: boil for
30 seconds and then remove from the heat.
Remove from the heat and whisk the caramel

and boiling milk together vigorously.
Spread the pears in the verrines, then cover with the cream
and leave to cool for at least 2 hours before serving.

APPLE TART CARAMEL SALTED BUTTER

very easy

Ingredients

2 apples
1 puff pastry
8 tablespoons of salted butterscotch caramel
2 teaspoons of powdered sugar
4 small jars of applesauce

Preparation

Place the puff pastry in a pie dish, pricking the bottom
with a fork.
Coat the bottom of the puff pastry with 3
or 4 tablespoons of caramel.
Pour the jars of compote on top.
Cut the apples into strips and arrange them
in a line on the compote.
Drop some caramel threads with a spoon
over the apples to coat them.
Sprinkle lightly with powdered sugar.
Preheat the oven 10 minutes before cooking and bake for
30 to 40 minutes (depending on the oven) at 200°c.

PAN-FRIED APPLES WITH CINNAMON AND ITS CARAMEL DEGLAZED WITH CREAM

very easy

Ingredients

2 apples
4 pinches of cinnamon
4 pieces of sugar
3 teaspoons of honey
1 water
10cl of fresh cream

Preparation

Empty the apples, then peel them.
Slice them into small pieces.
Put the sugar and honey in a hot pan.
Let it melt.
Add the water and let it caramelize.
Add the cream, stir well and remove from the heat.
Fry the apples with the cinnamon and remove from the heat.
Arrange the plate by putting the caramel on an apple dome.

Serve immediately.

APPLES AND PINE NUTS FRIED IN SALTED BUTTERSCOTCH CARAMEL

very easy

Ingredients

2 apples
50g of pinions
Butter
2 tablespoons of salted butterscotch caramel

Preparation

Peel and wash the apples.
Remove the core and cut into small pieces.
In a frying pan, melt a knob of butter over low heat
and add the apple pieces. Stir regularly.
When the apples are melting, add the pine nuts and
cook for another 5 minutes, taking care that the pine
nuts don't burn, then remove from the heat.
Just before serving, arrange the apples and pine nuts on plates
and add 1 tablespoon of salted butterscotch to each plate.
The caramel will melt on the hot apples!

IMPRINT

Mindful Publishing
We help you to publish your book!
By

TTENTION Inc.
Wilmington - DE19806
Trolley Square 20c

Instagram: mindful_publishing
Contact: mindful.publishing@web.de
Contact2: mindful.publishing@protonmail.com

Printed in Great Britain
by Amazon

23237039R00046